Highlights®

DINOSAURS
All Shapes and Sizes

By Dougal Dixon

CONTENTS

The Dinosaur series was created for Highlights for Children, Inc. by Bender Richardson White, P.O. Box 266, Uxbridge UB9 5NX, England

Printed in the USA

Project Editor: Lionel Bender
Art Director: Ben White
Production: Kim Richardson
Assistant Editor: Madeleine Samuel
Typesetting and Media Conversion: Peter MacDonald & Una Macnamara

Educational Advisor: Andrew Gutelle
Production Coordinator: Sarah Robinson

10 9 8 7 6 5 4

The Age of Dinosaurs
The first dinosaurs appeared about 225 million years ago (mya for short) in what scientists call the Late Triassic Period. They thrived through the following Jurassic Period, and died out at the end of the Cretaceous Period 65 million years ago. During this time, geography, climate, and vegetation, or plant life, were constantly changing—as shown in these dinosaur scenes.

Triassic 245–208 mya
A single giant landmass or supercontinent, mostly desert conditions, tree ferns, and conifers.

Early and Middle Jurassic 208–157 mya Supercontinent, shallow seas, moist climate, tree ferns, conifers, and cycads.

INTRODUCTION

"Dinosaurs!" Mention the word and what do we think about? Huge five-ton meat-eaters charging through dank forests, their huge claws ready to grab and kill any animal. Gigantic mountains or chunks of living tissue, lumbering slowly across the swamp, each with a tiny head on a long neck reaching for the leaves of tree ferns. Long-legged tree-eaters browsing the topmost branches. Reptilian tanks, coated with armor, bristling with spikes and horns.

What a spectacle! And indeed all these kinds of creatures did exist during the Age of Dinosaurs. Some of the dinosaurs were among the biggest land animals that walked the Earth. However, along with these there lived considerably smaller dinosaurs—little chicken-sized beasts that scuttled about in the undergrowth at the feet of the giants. There were also medium-sized dinosaurs, as big as pigs and sheep. They were all adapted to exist in particular ways in the landscapes of the times. These smaller dinosaurs showed all the dinosaur features to be found among the giants. They also displayed all kinds of other features that enabled them to live in totally different ways—as scavengers, as insect-eaters, as egg-stealers. The animal life of the Age of Dinosaurs was as varied and exciting as is the animal life of today.

Within the fact panel for each dinosaur we show a way of pronouncing the animal's name easily, and have listed the animal's most important features and where its remains have been found. A black oval on the little bar chart shows through which geological periods the animal lived. On the chart, mya is an abbreviation of *millions of years ago*. The drawing of the dinosaur is labeled to show the main body features. A scale diagram compares the size of the dinosaur to a 6-foot-tall person.

Late Jurassic 157–146 mya
Supercontinent beginning to break up, dry inland, moist climates by coasts.

Early Cretaceous 146–97 mya
Continents drifting into separate landmasses, plant life as in Triassic and Jurassic periods.

Late Cretaceous 97–65 mya
Separate continents, each with its own animal life, and plants like modern types.

COELOPHYSIS—hunting in packs

Like a wolf pack, the small group of agile creatures patters along the dry stream bed. Each one carries its big head low, its keen eyes looking ahead for food. The animals' slim bodies are each balanced on long birdlike hind legs by a stiff tail. They hold their strong-clawed hands folded close to the chest.

Coelophysis was one of the earliest hunting dinosaurs. Somewhere along this stream course lies their prey—one of the big hippopotamus-like plant-eating reptiles that died out in the Late Triassic Period as the dinosaurs took over.

We know that *Coelophysis* moved about in packs because a mass of their skeletons was found in a quarry in New Mexico. A whole pack must have died together. Maybe they were all washed away in a flash flood, or else they gathered round a water hole in a desert oasis until it dried up completely and they died of thirst. The second possibility seems likely, since some of the skeletons had the remains of baby *Coelophysis* in the stomach area. So harsh were the conditions that the adult dinosaurs were forced to eat the young of their own kind in order to survive.

In Connecticut, sandstone rocks from the Early Jurassic Period are full of the three-toed footprints of *Coelophysis,* or of some animal very similar. Before people knew anything about dinosaurs, these footprints were thought to have been made by birds of some kind.

COELOPHYSIS
SEE-lo-FY-sis

Length: Up to 9 feet.
Height: 22 inches at the hips.
Weight: 40 pounds.
Food: Small animals and possibly large plant-eaters.

Range: New Mexico. Very similar animals, but from Early Jurassic, in Arizona and Connecticut, and in Zimbabwe.

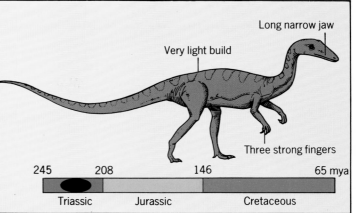

Long narrow jaw

Very light build

Three strong fingers

245	208	146	65 mya
Triassic	Jurassic	Cretaceous	

◁ The *Coelophysis* pack slinks along the dry stream bed as the startled flying reptile *Icarosaurus* glides away. *Coelophysis* had teeth like carving knives. Its narrow flexible snout allowed it to grab small active prey.

△ Modern wolves hunt their prey in packs, probably as *Coelophysis* did. A large pack can bring down prey bigger than any single wolf. Working alone, each wolf has to be content with catching small animals to eat.

HETERODONTOSAURUS—varied teeth

Most modern reptiles, such as lizards and crocodiles, have teeth that are all the same size. It is really only the mammals, such as cats, dogs, rodents, and monkeys, that have teeth organized into killing teeth, biting teeth, grinding teeth, and so on. Some of the dinosaurs, however, had different-sized teeth, each with special functions.

Heterodontosaurus (the name means "reptile with different-sized teeth") was one of the first of these. It had sharp teeth at the front for cutting off the leaves that it ate, long fangs at each side probably for breaking stems, and broad teeth at the back for grinding food. This is the same kind of tooth arrangement that people have! Some specimens seem to lack the fangs. Maybe only the males had them and they used them for fighting.

Apart from the teeth, *Heterodontosaurus* looked very much like any other primitive two-footed plant-eating dinosaur. It would have spent most of its time on its hind legs balanced by its long tail, like the meat-eaters of the time. If you had been around, you would easily have been able to tell a two-footed plant-eater from a meat-eater. The plant-eater would have had a much heavier body, as it needed a bigger intestine to digest its tough food. Also, nearly all the two-footed plant-eaters had cheek-pouches, to hold the food while chewing it. The meat-eaters would have had crocodile-like jaws. Like all the later two-footed plant-eaters, *Heterodontosaurus* had a horny beak at the front of its mouth. Its five-fingered hands had a big-clawed thumb that could grasp the plants on which it fed.

▷ With its teeth of different sizes, a *Heterodontosaurus* scavenges for food around a dead tree at the edge of the Early Jurassic desert.

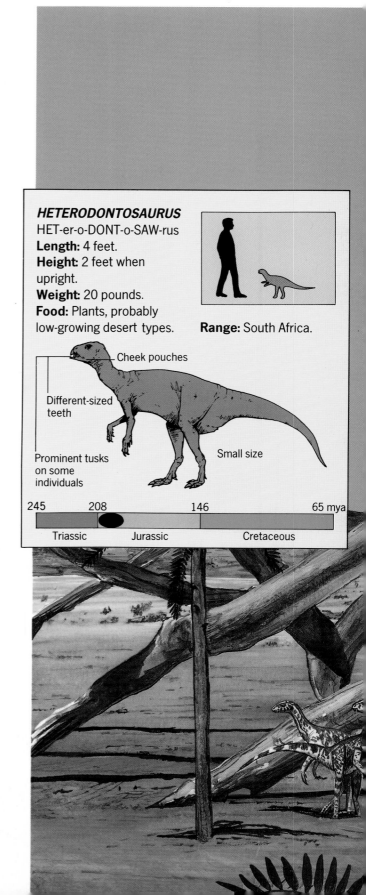

HETERODONTOSAURUS
HET-er-o-DONT-o-SAW-rus
Length: 4 feet.
Height: 2 feet when upright.
Weight: 20 pounds.
Food: Plants, probably low-growing desert types.
Range: South Africa.

Cheek pouches

Different-sized teeth

Prominent tusks on some individuals

Small size

245	208	146	65 mya
Triassic	Jurassic	Cretaceous	

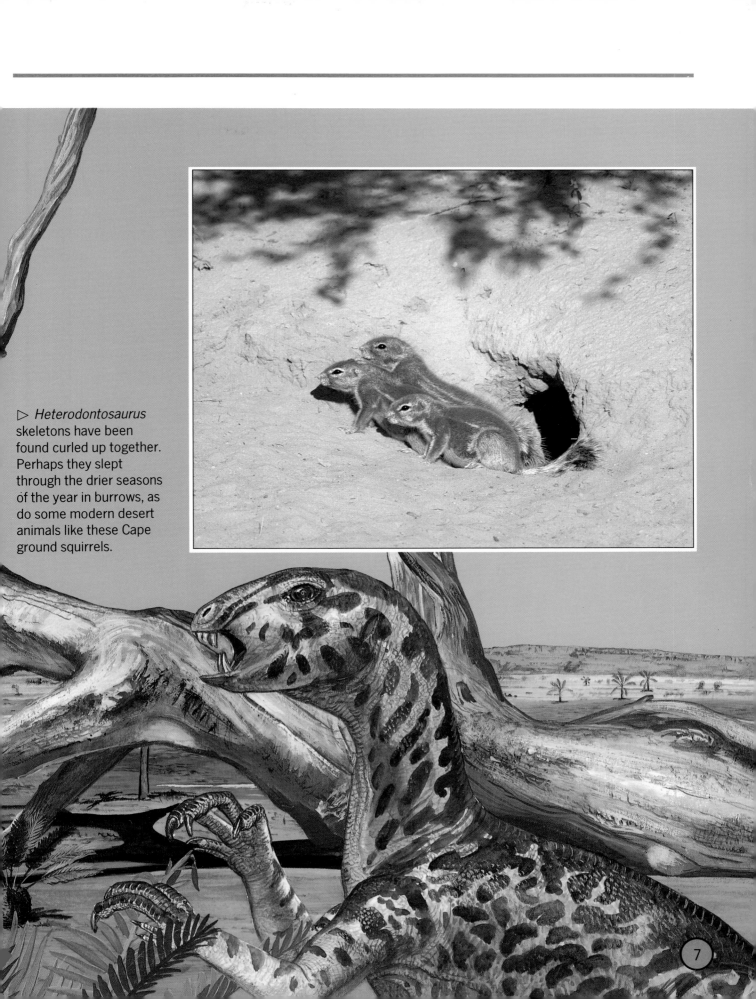

▷ *Heterodontosaurus* skeletons have been found curled up together. Perhaps they slept through the drier seasons of the year in burrows, as do some modern desert animals like these Cape ground squirrels.

SCUTELLOSAURUS—an armor coat

As the Age of Dinosaurs progressed, the plant-eating dinosaurs developed all kinds of techniques for escaping from the meat-eaters. Some became fast runners. Others became armored. *Scutellosaurus,* found in Early Jurassic rocks in North America, appears to be one of the first species that was both fast and armored.

It was lightly built, and although its hind legs were not as long as those of some other plant-eaters of the time, it was well balanced at the hips. Its tail was thin and very long— one and a half times the length of the rest of the body. *Scutellosaurus* could easily scamper away from danger. By comparison to the hind legs, the animal's forelimbs were quite long, so it looks as if *Scutellosaurus* spent most of its time down on all fours. It had tiny five-fingered clawed hands.

The most remarkable feature of this dinosaur was its armor. Parallel rows of bony studs covered its back and formed a spiky ridge from its skull to the tip of its tail. When attacked, *Scutellosaurus* may have crouched down in the soil presenting the armor to its attacker. Any large meat-eater that picked up the animal would get an extremely unpleasant bony mouthful.

Apart from these features, *Scutellosaurus* seems to have been very lizardlike. It was no bigger than some of the larger lizards that are alive today, and its head was quite unlike that of the other two-footed plant-eaters. It lacked the cheek pouches that most of the others had. Instead, it had widely spaced leaf-shaped teeth that it used to shred its plant food. Modern iguana lizards have similar teeth for exactly the same job.

▷ The long-tailed knobby *Scutellosaurus* surveys the landscape, keeping an eye open for enemies. If you saw it scuttling across dry rocks or disappearing into undergrowth, you would probably think that you were looking at some kind of lizard. *Scutellosaurus* means "reptile with little shields."

◁ In the modern world the armor of the pangolin probably comes closest to that of *Scutellosaurus*. Like the little dinosaur, the pangolin can run quite quickly when it is chased by a meat-eating animal. But if it is caught, its armor plates give it a great deal of protection.

SCUTELLOSAURUS
skoo-TELL-o-SAW-rus
Length: 4 feet.
Height: 1 foot at hips.
Weight: 20 pounds.

Food: Plants.
Range: Arizona.

Small size

Rows of bony plates

No cheek pouches

Strong forelimbs

Long tail

245	208	146	65 mya
Triassic	Jurassic	Cretaceous	

SCELIDOSAURUS—heavy and spiky

It is the Early Jurassic Period. A low upland ridge stretches across the area that now lies between Wales and Belgium. The vegetation that grows on the hills is the same green all over—the green of conifers and tree ferns. There are no flowers anywhere. At times big-headed *Dimorphodon* pterosaurs fly in the clear sky. In a valley, the ferns are pushed aside by a smallish knobbly-looking dinosaur, *Scelidosaurus,* as it lumbers down to the stream to drink.

Big meat-eating dinosaurs were around in Early Jurassic times. The plant-eaters had to beware and keep out of their way. At about this time the big plant-eaters began to develop armor. *Scelidosaurus* was one of the first of the species of armored dinosaurs.

At about the size of a sheep or small cow, *Scelidosaurus* was not really a big animal. However, it was obviously one that was too heavy to run away from its enemies. It used its armor to defend itself. The armor consisted of rows of bony knobs set into the skin of the back, running from the back of the skull down to the tip of the tail. In life, these knobs would have been sheathed in horn and were probably rather spiky. *Scelidosaurus* had legs that were fairly stout. It went around on all fours.

The main groups of armored dinosaurs did not evolve until the Late Jurassic and Early

SCELIDOSAURUS
skel-IDE-o-SAW-rus
Length: 13 feet.
Height: 3-4 feet at hips.
Weight: 500 pounds.

Food: Plants.
Range: Southern England, with closely related animals in Portugal and Germany.

Rows of conical plates on back

Beak

Cheek pouches

Four-footed stance

245	208	146	65 mya
Triassic	Jurassic	Cretaceous	

◁ The armored dinosaur *Scelidosaurus* approaches the Early Jurassic seashore. It would have carried its head close to the ground to feed on low-growing plants such as ferns, horsetails, and cycads.

Cretaceous periods. Scientists have always thought that *Scelidosaurus* must have been the ancestor of the later types. The two great armored groups were the stegosaurs, with upright plates and spines on the back, and the ankylosaurs, with horizontal shields and spikes pointing out sideways. It seems most likely that *Scelidosaurus* belonged to a group that evolved into the ankylosaurs. One reason for this thinking is that *Scelidosaurus* had its skull encased in bony plates, as had the later ankylosaurs but not the stegosaurs. But we have found no fossils of armored dinosaurs from the 40 million years between *Scelidosaurus* and the later armored types.

▽ The Indian rhinoceros is a large, armored, stoutly built plant-eater. Its armor consists of thick folds of lumpy skin. It relies on its armor in battles with other rhinoceroses for territory or for mates.

ORNITHOLESTES—a small, swift hunter

On the Late Jurassic plains of western North America, herds of huge plant-eaters like *Apatosaurus* and *Brachiosaurus,* and the armored giants like *Stegosaurus,* were stalked and killed by mighty meat-eaters, among them *Allosaurus*. However, not all the dinosaurs there at that time were large monsters. There were also lightweight, nimble little meat-eaters like *Ornitholestes*.

The small mammals of the time, along with the lizards and lizardlike animals, and even hatchling dinosaurs, would have been fair game for any small jackal-sized hunter. *Ornitholestes* was just such a creature, and its light build would also have given it the speed to chase down startled lizards or to escape from enraged adult dinosaurs who found their nests raided.

Ornitholestes had a body shape like that of the big meat-eaters but on a small scale. In fact, it was probably closely related to the local giant, *Allosaurus*. It could use its hands well. Each hand had two very long fingers and one quite short. *Ornitholestes* could probably have used the short finger like a thumb for grasping. All three fingers had strong claws.

The skull of *Ornitholestes* was very short, which is unusual for the smaller meat-eating dinosaurs, and its lower jaw was deep and strong. This may mean that the animal killed its prey by a strong bite, as do cats, rather than by pulling it to bits with its claws.

Ornitholestes means "bird-robber," but there is no evidence to show that it really did catch and eat birds.

△ The modern secretary bird of Africa is like *Ornitholestes*. It is a swift long-legged ground hunter that chases small mammals and reptiles through the undergrowth in the same way that we believe *Ornitholestes* did in Jurassic times.

ORNITHOLESTES
or-NITH-o-LESS-teez
Length: 6 feet.
Height: 16 inches at hips.
Weight: 25 pounds.
Food: Meat—probably small living things caught on the run, maybe carrion.
Range: Wyoming.

Small crest

Two grasping fingers and a thumb

Small size

245	208	146	65 mya
Triassic	Jurassic	Cretaceous	

◁ *Ornitholestes* snatches a young crocodile from its nest to eat. Having killed its prey, *Ornitholestes* probably swallowed it whole. *Ornitholestes*'s small size meant that it could hunt small fast-moving prey that was not available to the larger dinosaurs of the region.

ELAPHROSAURUS—a birdlike meat-eater

This dinosaur was like a cheetah—long and lean, built for speed—but it ran on its hind legs. It lived on the wooded coastal plain of Tanzania in East Africa in the Late Jurassic Period. Its neighbors were the huge long-necked plant-eater *Brachiosaurus* and the stegosaur *Kentrosaurus*. These it left well alone. Instead, it hunted the small or medium-sized plant-eaters such as *Dryosaurus,* a close relative of *Hypsilophodon.*

The lightness of *Elaphrosaurus*'s build and parts of its skeleton, particularly the front limbs, make us think that it was related to the small meat-eating dinosaurs of Triassic and Early Jurassic times, such as *Coelophysis.*

However, its size and its leg bones seem to show that it was an early member of the birdlike dinosaurs, such as *Avimimus,* which became common later.

An incomplete skeleton was discovered in Tanzania in the 1920s. Since then, odd bones possibly from *Elaphrosaurus* have been found all over northern Africa. In the 1980s, an arm bone that seems to have belonged to a front limb of this beast was found in Late Jurassic rocks of Wyoming in the United States. This suggests that *Elaphrosaurus,* as well as *Brachiosaurus* and the stegosaurs, spread all over the world before the continents broke up in the middle of the Age of Dinosaurs.

▽ Long-bodied, swift-moving *Elaphrosaurus* must have pursued the agile plant-eater *Dryosaurus* through the woods and thickets of Late Jurassic Tanzania, dodging to keep its prey in sight as it ran it down.

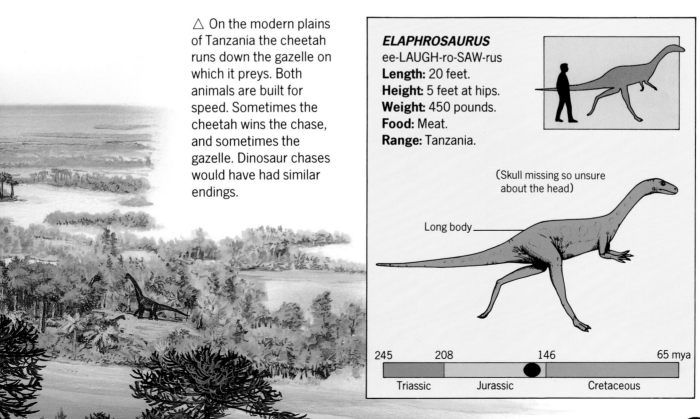

△ On the modern plains of Tanzania the cheetah runs down the gazelle on which it preys. Both animals are built for speed. Sometimes the cheetah wins the chase, and sometimes the gazelle. Dinosaur chases would have had similar endings.

ELAPHROSAURUS
ee-LAUGH-ro-SAW-rus
Length: 20 feet.
Height: 5 feet at hips.
Weight: 450 pounds.
Food: Meat.
Range: Tanzania.

(Skull missing so unsure about the head)

Long body

245	208	146	65 mya
Triassic	Jurassic	Cretaceous	

KENTROSAURUS—with unusual features

When we think of stegosaurs, we usually picture the massive *Stegosaurus* itself. However, the stegosaurs were a group of dinosaurs of various shapes and sizes. Some of them were quite small. *Kentrosaurus* was only about the size of a large cow. But it was not only its size that was special. The arrangement of plates on its back was totally different from that of *Stegosaurus*. Instead of a double row of broad slabs, *Kentrosaurus* had plates that were so narrow they could be considered spines. Its name means "pointy reptile." Small and leaflike over the neck, the spines grew tall and narrow over the hips and tail. There was also a pair of sideways-pointing spines in the region of the hips or shoulders.

Scientists disagree over the exact purpose of the stegosaurs' plates or spines. Many think that the big broad plates of *Stegosaurus* were used for controlling the heat of the animal. The plates and spines of *Kentrosaurus* would seem to be far too narrow for this job. Maybe *Kentrosaurus*'s smaller size meant that it did not need such a complicated temperature control system. Its plates and spines were probably used only as armor. Only when the big stegosaurs, like *Stegosaurus,* evolved, did these armor spines develop into heat exchangers.

A second brain or a powerpack?
Another dinosaur feature that experts disagree about is a cavity, or hollow space, that lies between the hip bones of the stegosaurs. It was once thought that this housed a second brain that could control movement of the hind legs and the tail. It is more likely to have held a gland or organ—a mass of body tissue—that supplied energy to the hindparts of the animal in an emergency.

▷ *Kentrosaurus* browses in the thicket, protected from the fierce meat-eaters of the time by its bladelike plates and sharp spines. Scientists at first thought the sideways-pointing spines were over the hip, but discoveries in China have shown that they were over the shoulder as shown here. *Kentrosaurus* lived in the wooded riversides of Tanzania in Late Jurassic times.

KENTROSAURUS
KENT-ro-SAW-rus
Length: up to 15 feet.
Height: 3-6 feet.

Weight: 1,000 pounds.
Food: Plants.
Range: Tanzania.

Narrow plates on neck and back

Small head

Beak

Cheek pouches

Long spines on tail

245   208   146   65 mya

Triassic   Jurassic   Cretaceous

COMPSOGNATHUS—lizard-chaser

A little chicken-sized creature, scampering along a shoreline, disturbing clouds of sandflies from the mounds of seaweed.

Not the image we usually have of a dinosaur, is it? Yet this is *Compsognathus,* the smallest and lightest dinosaur that we know. It must have looked very much like a naked chicken. In build and structure it was very much like the first bird, *Archaeopteryx,* which lived at the same time and in the same place. This was the Late Jurassic, and the place was the island group that lay scattered across the shallow sea that covered much of northern Europe at that time.

The skeletons of *Compsognathus* discovered so far exist as fossils in well-formed limestone rock that developed in shallow waters long ago. The limestone was formed so perfectly that it has preserved details of the dinosaur's way of life. The most famous skeleton, found in Germany, is possibly that of a female. It still had the bones of the animal's last meal in its stomach cavity. It was a fast-moving long-tailed lizard like a modern iguana. *Compsognathus* probably ate other small animals, too, such as insects and early mammals.

Now we can picture its last activities. While searching for somewhere to lay her eggs, the *Compsognathus* sees the lizard run out into the sunlight of the beach. This is too good a chance of a meal to miss. On her long hind legs she scampers after it and, after a short chase, she seizes it in her little teeth, kills it, and swallows it whole. Maybe the chase took her so far down the beach that a wave caught her and she drowned. Eventually she sank to the bottom of the sea and was fossilized.

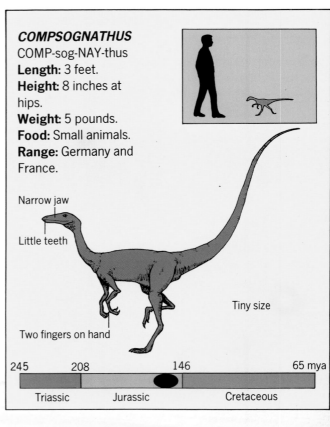

COMPSOGNATHUS
COMP-sog-NAY-thus
Length: 3 feet.
Height: 8 inches at hips.
Weight: 5 pounds.
Food: Small animals.
Range: Germany and France.

Narrow jaw

Little teeth

Two fingers on hand

Tiny size

245	208	146	65 mya
Triassic	Jurassic	Cretaceous	

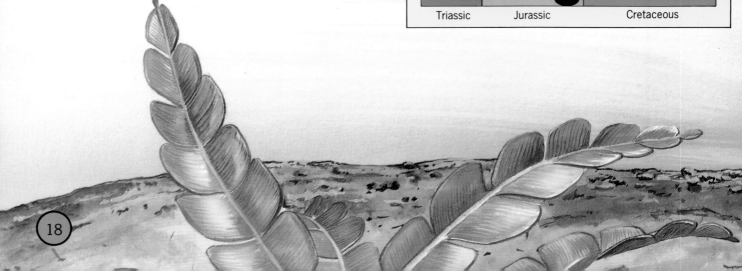

▽ Imagine a chicken without any feathers. Then give it a long tail and a toothy mouth. This is what *Compsognathus* looked like. One skeleton of the first bird, *Archaeopteryx*, was thought to have been that of *Compsognathus* until someone noticed there were impressions of feathers around it.

HYPSILOPHODON—small but speedy

A small plant-eating dinosaur, built for speed so that it could escape the big meat-eaters by running away across open ground. That describes *Hypsilophodon*. For a plant-eater it was very lightly built and well-balanced at the hips. The legs were long and graceful, with short thighs and particularly long shin bones and toes. Most of the leg muscles worked on the short thigh bone. This meant that all the weight was concentrated at the thigh and the hip, and the rest of the leg was lightweight. An arrangement like this meant that the legs could be moved quickly, showing that *Hypsilophodon* was a running animal.

Apart from that, *Hypsilophodon* must have looked like a little *Iguanodon,* the classic big plant-eating dinosaur of Early Cretaceous southern England. A sharp narrow beak would have allowed *Hypsilophodon* to select and nip out the tastiest pieces from the shoots and leaves on which it fed. It would have used its chisel-like cheek teeth to chop up the food while holding it in its cheek pouches.

The arms of *Hypsilophodon* were quite long, although shorter than the legs, with hands each having five stubby fingers. These would have been ideal for grabbing and pulling food toward the mouth. Like most two-footed dinosaurs, *Hypsilophodon* had a long tail that was stiffened by bony tendons and held straight out behind. It was used as a balancing pole while running.

On the Isle of Wight, off southern England, is a layer of rock packed with *Hypsilophodon* skeletons. Evidently a disaster overcame a herd of them. Probably they were crossing coastal mudflats and were cut off by the tide, or they were trapped in quicksand. Whatever killed them was something they could not run away from fast enough.

HYPSILOPHODON

hip-see-LOAF-o-don
Length: 7 feet.
Height: 3 feet at hips.
Weight: 50 pounds.

Food: Leaves and shoots of low-growing plants.
Range: Southern England.

Beak

Cheek pouches

Five fingers

Light build

Running legs with short thighs and long shanks

245	208	146	65 mya
Triassic	Jurassic	Cretaceous	

▽ A group of *Hypsilophodon* trudges along in the rain. *Hypsilophodon* would have looked like the dinosaur equivalent of the gazelle. It was about the same size, and its legs were built the same way.

PSITTACOSAURUS—tough bones and beak

The head of *Psittacosaurus* was narrow and square, and had a huge beak. It looked just like the head of a parrot. That is where its name comes from: *Psittacosaurus* means "parrot-reptile." The square shape to the head was due to a ridge of bone around the back of the skull. This anchored the strong jaw muscles that gave the big beak its powerful bite. Otherwise the body looked like that of the other small two-footed plant-eaters, such as *Hypsilophodon*.

Scientists think that *Psittacosaurus* belonged to a group of dinosaurs that evolved into the big-horned dinosaurs of the end of the Cretaceous Period. We can see how this came about. As the body became bigger, the animal would have gone down on all fours, bringing the head closer to the low-growing plants on which it fed. The bone arrangement in the beak is the same as that in the beaks of the horned dinosaurs. The ridge at the back of the skull would have expanded to become a frill of armor or a kind of display structure.

Some species of *Psittacosaurus* had a broad head with spines growing sideways from the cheek bones. These spines could easily have developed into horns for defense. One kind had a tiny nasal horn. It had become a typical horned dinosaur, like *Triceratops*.

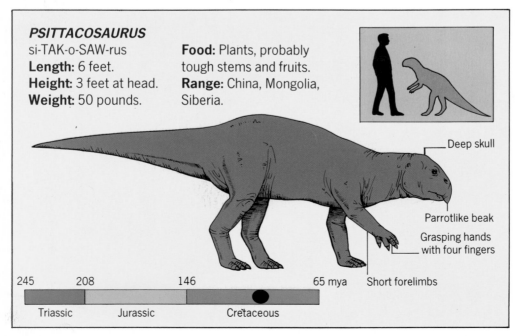

PSITTACOSAURUS
si-TAK-o-SAW-rus
Length: 6 feet.
Height: 3 feet at head.
Weight: 50 pounds.

Food: Plants, probably tough stems and fruits.
Range: China, Mongolia, Siberia.

Deep skull

Parrotlike beak

Grasping hands with four fingers

Short forelimbs

245	208	146	65 mya
Triassic	Jurassic	Cretaceous	

△ The beak of a modern parrot is a powerful tool. The bird can use it to break through the shells of tough nuts. By working its strong tongue along inside the beak, the parrot can move food about in its mouth. Maybe *Psittacosaurus* had such a tongue?

▷ *Psittacosaurus* selects leaves and fruit for its food. The huge beak and the strong jaw muscles of this small dinosaur enabled it to bite into the hardest of plant materials.

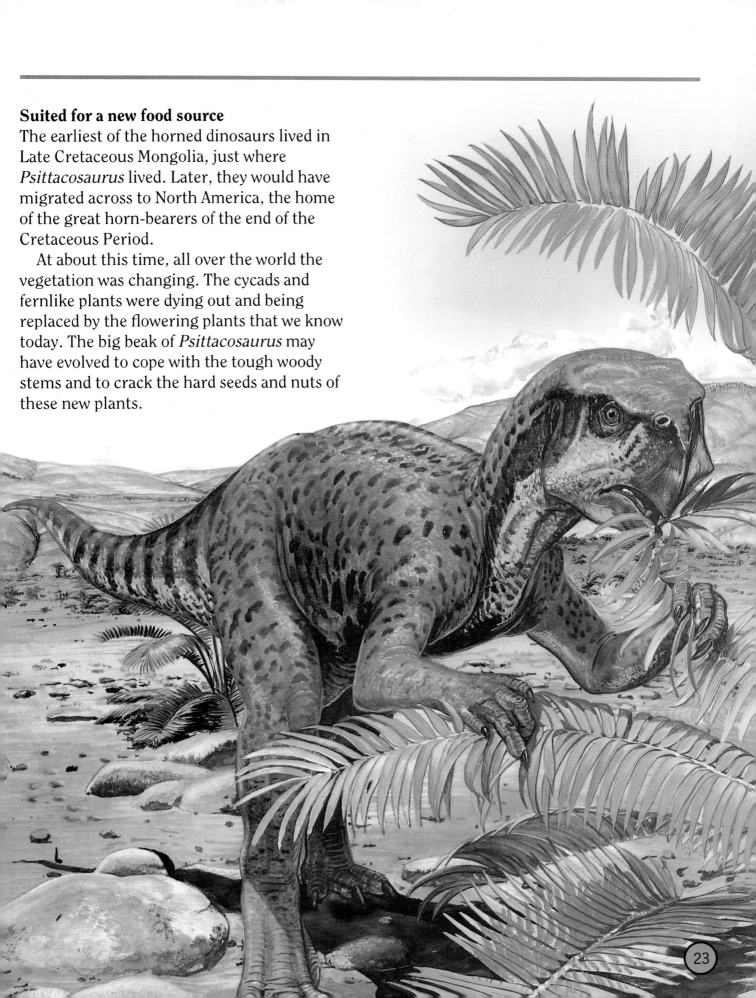

Suited for a new food source

The earliest of the horned dinosaurs lived in Late Cretaceous Mongolia, just where *Psittacosaurus* lived. Later, they would have migrated across to North America, the home of the great horn-bearers of the end of the Cretaceous Period.

At about this time, all over the world the vegetation was changing. The cycads and fernlike plants were dying out and being replaced by the flowering plants that we know today. The big beak of *Psittacosaurus* may have evolved to cope with the tough woody stems and to crack the hard seeds and nuts of these new plants.

STYGIMOLOCH—herd-living bonehead

Imagine this dinosaur popping its head up through the undergrowth to look at you! A head as big as a soccer ball, with a dome on top and surrounded by spikes and horns. Yet, like most other alarming-looking animals, *Stygimoloch* was a harmless plant-eater.

It was a member of a group of dinosaurs that we call the boneheads. These were mostly sheep-sized animals, although the biggest species grew to about 25 feet long. In bodily build they were much like the usual two-footed plant-eaters. But in the structure of the head, they were quite different. The top of the skull was very thick. In some species, including *Stygimoloch,* this thickening was enlarged into a distinct dome. It must have seemed as if each animal's skull contained a large brain. However, it was nearly all bone, and bone that was thickened in such a way as to make it extemely strong.

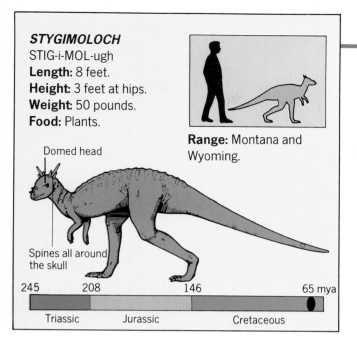

STYGIMOLOCH
STIG-i-MOL-ugh
Length: 8 feet.
Height: 3 feet at hips.
Weight: 50 pounds.
Food: Plants.

Range: Montana and Wyoming.

Domed head

Spines all around the skull

245	208	146	65 mya
Triassic	Jurassic	Cretaceous	

◁ A male *Stygimoloch* rests in the shade after a head-butting contest with another male. Dome-headed dinosaurs probably had such fights to decide who would lead the herd, just as male mountain goats do today. The boneheads may also have been mountain dwellers. Most of their remains that we know consist of skulls that had been washed down from the mountains and badly worn by water before being fossilized.

▽ The modern horned lizard, the so-called horned toad, has spines around its head as did *Stygimoloch*. Like the lizard's, the spines of *Stygimoloch* may have kept off meat-eaters.

Little brains, lots of brawn

What would a dome on the head have been used for? It seems likely that the boneheads lived in herds, and that the big males fought for leadership of the herds by head-butting one another, just as male sheep and goats do today. The bones of the neck and back were arranged to withstand the shock when the head was used as a battering ram. In *Stygimoloch,* the domed head was surrounded by spines, no doubt to make the head look bigger and more frightening. (To us it may have looked like some sort of monster.) Perhaps *Stygimoloch* rivals did not charge and crash with one another but instead locked horns and pushed.

The hips of the boneheads were very wide, and it is possible that this means these species of dinosaurs gave birth to live young rather than laying eggs.

OVIRAPTOR—fierce and fast egg-robber

Do you eat eggs for breakfast? There is plenty of protein in an egg—good nourishing food. Most of the dinosaurs laid eggs, and so during dinosaur times there must have been a great number of good meals lying around in the form of eggs. One feature of evolution is that wherever there is a new food supply, something will evolve to feed on it. We think that *Oviraptor* was a dinosaur that evolved to eat the eggs of others.

The first skeleton of an *Oviraptor* to be found was lying near a nest full of eggs of *Protoceratops,* one of the first horned dinosaurs. The animal must have been buried in a sandstorm while it was robbing the nest.

The head of *Oviraptor* was very odd. The skull was extremely short with a deep beak.

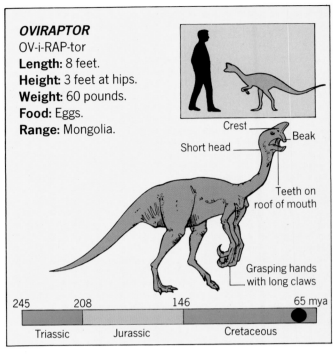

OVIRAPTOR
OV-i-RAP-tor
Length: 8 feet.
Height: 3 feet at hips.
Weight: 60 pounds.
Food: Eggs.
Range: Mongolia.

Crest
Beak
Short head
Teeth on roof of mouth
Grasping hands with long claws

245   208   146   65 mya

Triassic   Jurassic   Cretaceous

△ There are birds around today that eat the eggs of others, like this crow about to eat a goose's egg. We know this because we see it happen. When it comes to dinosaurs, though, we can get an idea of what they ate by the shapes of the mouth and teeth.

The only teeth were a pair high up on the roof of the mouth. A mouth of this shape would have been perfect for cracking open eggs. *Oviraptor* had a tall crest just like that of a cassowary, a bird that lives today in Australia and New Guinea. The eyes were at each side of the head, to allow it to keep a lookout all round for danger while it fed. The hands were short, with three strong-clawed fingers shaped so that they could hold big eggs.

The body of *Oviraptor* was built like that of the small meat-eating dinosaurs, so that it would have looked a lot like a large bird. The long legs would have allowed it to run off when danger threatened, but the big claws and the strong beak would have been formidable weapons if it came to a fight.

▷ Crouched over a dinosaur nest by moonlight, *Oviraptor* watches for the owner. *Oviraptor* evolved as an egg-eater. With its flexible hands it could hold an egg while using its deep beak and special teeth to break through the shell. It then gobbled up the contents.

AVIMIMUS— built like a bird

Avimimus, or "bird-mimic," was the most birdlike of all dinosaurs. The eyes were big, like an owl's. The skull was deep and narrow, like a pheasant's. The legs were long, resembling those of a roadrunner; the toes were short like an ostrich's. The arms could be tucked back against the body, just as wings can. In fact, the whole beast was so birdlike that some paleontologists think that it evolved from the first types of birds, or at least some earlier flying creature. They show the dinosaur covered with feathers. It was no bird, though.

The hips of *Avimimus* were typical dinosaur hips and its arms were too small to have been wings. The tail is missing from the only known skeleton of *Avimimus,* and some scientists think that it did not have a proper tail at all, just a bunch of long feathers as birds do. But most others do not believe this since the hips are very broad and show where strong tail muscles were attached.

Although *Avimimus* was related to the small meat-eating dinosaurs, it seems more likely that it ate plants. This is similar to the way that bears and pandas are related to the

◁ The modern roadrunner has a pair of legs similar in structure and shape to those of *Avimimus.* It can fly, but prefers to run, just as the smaller dinosaurs did.

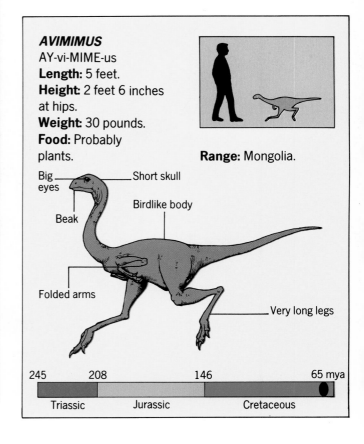

AVIMIMUS
AY-vi-MIME-us
Length: 5 feet.
Height: 2 feet 6 inches at hips.
Weight: 30 pounds.
Food: Probably plants.

Range: Mongolia.

Big eyes — Short skull

Beak — Birdlike body

Folded arms

Very long legs

245	208	146	65 mya
Triassic	Jurassic	Cretaceous	

meat-eating dogs and cats, but they eat mostly plants. *Avimimus* had a completely different diet from its cousins. Its broad beak, like that of an ostrich, seems to have been adapted for eating low-growing vegetable matter. The long ostrichlike neck would have allowed it to reach down to the ground. A saw edge on the beak enabled it to remove plants easily from the soil.

It was clearly a running animal with legs as long as its body and neck. It must have grazed on open plains and taken to its heels as soon as one of its meat-eating relatives appeared.

Avimimus lived on the open plains of Late Cretaceous Mongolia. There, at the same time, lived the egg-stealer *Oviraptor*. There were also small meat-eaters that were fast on their feet and armed with killing claws. Such animals as *Troodon* and *Velociraptor* would have given chase, but *Avimimus* would have given them a good run.

▽ *Avimimus* sprints across the Late Cretaceous plains of central Asia, its head bobbing and its arms tucked into its body. Built for speed, it would have outrun most of the meat-eating hunting dinosaurs of the time.

DO YOU KNOW?

Which was the smallest dinosaur?
The little meat-eater *Compsognathus*, with a length of 3 feet and a weight of 5 pounds, is thought of as the smallest dinosaur. Remains of a shorter dinosaur found in Colorado was a two-footed plant-eater related to *Scutellosaurus* but without the armor. It probably weighed about 15 pounds but was only about 2½ feet long.

Which is the smallest baby dinosaur known?
Nests of *Orodromeus*—a plant-eater like *Hypsilophodon*—lie in rocks in Montana. One of the eggs contains an embryo that is 4 inches long. The skeleton of a young *Mussaurus* has been found that is 8 inches long but its tail is missing.

Did any dinosaur climb trees?
Scientists used to believe that *Hypsilophodon* climbed trees. This was because it was built like the modern tree kangaroo and the foot bones seemed to have been adapted to perching. We now know that this was not the case. *Hypsilophodon* was a sprinter.

Which was the most intelligent dinosaur?
What may have been the most intelligent dinosaur was *Troodon* from Late Cretaceous Canada. It was a small meat-eater, and it had a brain as big as that of some of today's birds.

Which was the fastest dinosaur?
A little dinosaur living in Arizona in the Early Jurassic Period left intriguing footprints in the rocks. The animal weighed about 20 pounds and yet made footprints that were about 12 feet apart. Scientists have worked out that the animal must have been running at 40 miles an hour.

Which was the smallest armored dinosaur?
Struthiosaurus from Late Cretaceous eastern Europe was an armored dinosaur that was only about 6 feet long.

Which was the most birdlike dinosaur?
Avimimus, whose name means "bird mimic," had a skeleton that was so birdlike that some scientists think it was covered with feathers and could fly.

Which was the last-surviving plated dinosaur?
Dravidosaurus, a relative of *Stegosaurus*, lived in India in the Late Cretaceous Period. All other stegosaurs died out in Jurassic or Early Cretaceous times. *Dravidosaurus*, which is the only stegosaur known from India, may have lived on there because India was an island at the time, as Australia is now, and there may have been few of its enemies around.

Which was the smallest horned dinosaur?
This was *Microceratops*—"tiny horned face"—from Late Cretaceous China. It was about 30 inches long and was built like *Hypsilophodon*, but it had a tiny nose horn and neck frill.

What was the smallest tyrannosaur?
We think of the tyrannosaurs, such as *Tyrannosaurus*, as being the biggest of the meat-eaters. However, there were smaller types as well. *Nanotyrannus*, from Late Cretaceous Montana, was only 15 feet long.

Which dinosaur had the biggest eyes?
Dromiceiomimus, a relative of *Troodon*, had eyes which were about 3 inches in diameter.

GLOSSARY

beak a horny mouth structure that occurs on birds and some dinosaurs. It is more lightweight than a set of teeth but is used in the same way.

browses feeds on shoots, leaves, and bark of shrubs and trees.

cheek pouches folds of skin and muscle at the sides of the mouth that hold food while chewing.

conifers trees that produce seeds in cones—for example, pines, firs, and larches. Their needlelike leaves usually stay on the trees all year.

crest a structure on top of the head, usually for display.

Cretaceous the period of geological time between 146 and 65 million years ago. It was the end of the Age of Dinosaurs.

cycads plants related to the conifers consisting of a thick trunk and a bunch of palmlike leaves.

evolve to change over many generations, producing a new species.

fangs long pointed teeth.

ferns nonflowering plants with finely divided leaves known as fronds.

flash flood a sudden rush of water down a river valley following rainfall in nearby mountains.

fossilized turned into fossils.

fossils parts or traces of once-living plants or animals that are preserved in the rocks.

grazed to have eaten low-growing plants. Modern grazers eat grass and include sheep, goats, and cattle.

horn a tough shiny substance composed of the same chemical material as hair. Horn often forms as a protective covering on some part of an animal. The word horn is also used for a structure covered with the material, like that of a cow.

horsetails plants, related to ferns, with sprays of green branches along an upright stem, and tiny leaves.

intestine the part of the food canal beyond the stomach in which the nutrients are taken up by the body.

Jurassic the period of geological time between 208 and 146 million years ago. It is the middle period of the Age of Dinosaurs.

limestone a rock made up mostly of calcium carbonate and formed in water. Limestone is usually made up of very fine grains.

mammals vertebrate (backboned) animals that produce live young and feed them on milk. Modern mammals include cats, dogs, mice, rabbits, whales, monkeys, and ourselves.

migrated moved from place to place as conditions changed to find new sources of food or shelter or to mate and bring up young.

paleontologists people who study paleontology, the science of ancient life and fossils.

prehistoric in ancient times; before written historical records.

pterosaurs members of a group of flying reptiles related to the dinosaurs that flew using a wing of skin during the Triassic, Jurassic, and Cretaceous periods.

quicksand an area of wet sand that may become almost liquid when stepped on. Swallows up anything that walks on it.

reptiles vertebrate animals generally with a dry, scaly skin that lay shelled eggs. Living reptiles include lizards and turtles.

scavenge to feed on the dead bodies of other animals.

species a collection of animals, or any living things, in which individuals look like one another and can breed with each other to produce young. Breeding, reproduction, and mating are all terms to describe the process by which individuals make more of their species.

tendons tough pieces of animal tissue that attach the muscles to the bones.

tree ferns plants of the fern family that grow to over 80 feet in height. There are only a few living species, but they were plentiful at the beginning of the Age of Dinosaurs.

Triassic the period of geological time between 245 and 208 million years ago. The dinosaurs first evolved in the Triassic Period.

vertebrates animals that have a backbone. This includes the fish, amphibians, reptiles, birds, and mammals. As mammals, we are also vertebrates.

INDEX

ACKNOWLEDGMENTS

Picture credits
Page 5 Udo Hirsch/Bruce Coleman Limited. Page 7 K.G.
Preston-Mafham/Premaphotos Wildlife. Page 8 Keith and Liz Laidler/Ardea
London Limited. Pages 11, 13, K.G. Preston-Mafham/Premaphotos Wildlife.
Page 15 J.J. Brooks/Aquila Photographics. Page 22 Partridge Films
Ltd/Oxford Scientific Films. Page 25 Michael Fogden/Oxford Scientific
Films. Page 26 Hans Reinhard/Bruce Coleman Limited. Page 28 Bob
Langrish/Frank Lane Photo Agency.

Artwork credits
All major color illustrations, including the cover, by Steve Kirk.
All diagrammatic artwork by Hayward Art Group.
Chris Forsey: pages 1, 2-3.